Sea Turtles and Yellow Tang Fish

By Kevin Cunningham

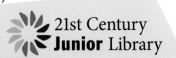

21st Century
Junior Library

Published in the United States of America by
Cherry Lake Publishing
Ann Arbor, Michigan
www.cherrylakepublishing.com

Content Adviser: Stephen Ditchkoff, Professor of Wildlife Ecology and Management, Auburn University, Alabama
Reading Adviser: Marla Conn MS, Ed., Literacy specialist, Read-Ability, Inc.

Photo Credits: © Marty Wakat/Shutterstock, cover, 1, 10, 12, 18, 20; © idreamphoto/Shutterstock, 4;
© Mike Bauer/Shutterstock, 6; © Melissa Brandes/Shutterstock, 8; © mexrix/Shutterstock, 14;
© Jonathan R. Green | Dreamstime.com, 16

Library of Congress Cataloging-in-Publication Data

Names: Cunningham, Kevin, 1966- author.
Title: Sea turtles and Yellow Tang fish / Kevin Cunningham.
Description: Ann Arbor, MI : Cherry Lake Publishing, [2016] | Series: Better together |
    Audience: K to grade 3. | Includes bibliographical references and index.
Identifiers: LCCN 2015049542 | ISBN 9781634710886 (hardcover) | ISBN 9781634712866 (pbk.) |
    ISBN 9781634711876 (pdf) | ISBN 9781634713856 (ebook)
Subjects: LCSH: Mutualism (Biology)—Juvenile literature. | Green turtle—Juvenile literature. |
    Animal behavior—Juvenile literature.
Classification: LCC QH548.3 .C867 2016 | DDC 591.7/85—dc23
LC record available at http://lccn.loc.gov/2015049542

Cherry Lake Publishing would like to acknowledge the work of The Partnership for 21st Century Skills.
Please visit *www.p21.org* for more information.

Printed in the United States of America
Corporate Graphics

CONTENTS

Green sea turtles are native to the warm waters around Hawaii.

The Honu

Native people in Hawaii call the green sea turtle the *honu*. Kauila, a magical honu, lived inside a **spring**. The island people used the spring for **fresh water**. When it bubbled, they said, Kauila was sleeping. Kauila sometimes turned into a little girl. She watched over the human children nearby. She helped humans.

These two sea creatures make a great team.

Other creatures help the green sea turtle. The yellow tang fish and the honu teamed up long ago.

Look!

Find a picture of a green sea turtle. How does its body seem built to swim? Why would its flat shape help with swimming? What does the green sea turtle have instead of legs?

Sea turtles lay their eggs on sandy beaches like this one.

Big Turtle

Sea turtles are **reptiles**. They are different from the turtles we see on land. For one thing, they're huge. An adult green sea turtle weighs between 200 and 450 pounds (91 and 204 kilograms). The largest ones grow to over 800 pounds (363 kg).

A green sea turtle cannot tuck its head into its shell. It is also the only kind of sea turtle that relaxes on land. It likes to live in

Sea turtles will migrate hundreds—or even thousands—of miles each year.

the **tropics**. The weather stays warm there. The turtles get many chances to sunbathe.

Green sea turtles have few natural **predators**. A healthy green sea turtle lives 50 years or more. Some may reach 80 years old. But they need help from a fish to celebrate all those birthdays.

Yellow tang fish can grow up to 7.9 inches (20 centimeters) long.

Algae Problem

Yellow tang fish travel in small groups. They usually stay in the top 100 feet (30.5 meters) of water in the ocean. A yellow tang fish keeps its bright color during the day. At night, it turns gray-yellow. Changing color helps it hide from predators.

The yellow tang fish swims in a **coral reef**. It darts here and there. Its **oval**-shaped body sometimes disappears into

Coral reefs are found in warm coastal waters all over the world.
They are home to many sea creatures.

a hole. Plants called algae grow inside. The yellow tang fish loves algae. The fish has tiny teeth. It bites off pieces of algae to eat.

Algae grow like crazy. They even grow on the shells of green sea turtles. A green sea turtle with algae on its shell is in danger. The algae cause **drag**. That keeps the green sea turtle from swimming fast. A predator can catch and eat a slow green sea turtle.

Green sea turtles know that algae put them in danger. They also know they have

A sea turtle's large size and heavy shell help protect it from predators. But algae growing on its shell will slow the sea turtle down.

an **ally**. The algae may grow thick on a sea turtle's shell. But the yellow tang fish is there to help.

Make a Guess!

A green sea turtle can swim 20 miles (32 kilometers) per hour. It also lives under a hard shell. What kind of predator might be able to catch and eat a green sea turtle?

Yellow tang fish are like nature's car wash.

Cleaning Station

A yellow tang fish eats all the time. It cleans algae off the reef. That keeps the reef healthy.

Green sea turtles often swim around coral reefs. Yellow tang fish aren't afraid of these reptiles. Green sea turtles eat plants, not fish.

A green sea turtle swims toward the reef. Yellow tang fish wait there. The turtle

The partnership between the yellow tang fish and the
green sea turtle is important for the survival of both animals.

stops at the **cleaning station**. It floats. The yellow tang fish get to work. They eat algae off the turtle's shell.

The yellow tang fish eat a good meal. Their ally, the green sea turtle, gets its shell clean. The turtle can swim at top speed again. It can leave predators behind. Each animal has helped the other.

Ask Questions!

Many people call algae a weed (even though algae is not a plant!). Weeds grow everywhere. Ask a teacher, parent, or other adult why we get rid of weeds. Why do you think coral reefs need animals to eat up algae? What might happen to the reef if algae grew all over it?

GLOSSARY

ally (AL-eye) a creature that helps another creature

cleaning station (KLEEN-ing STAY-shun) a place where yellow tang fish clean green sea turtles

coral reef (KOR-uhl REEF) a great mass of tiny living organisms and their hard outer shells that have built up over time

drag (DRAG) something that slows down an animal

fresh water (FRESH WAH-tur) water without salt in it

oval (OH-vuhl) shaped like an egg

predators (PRED-uh-turz) animals that hunt other animals for food

reptiles (REP-tylz) a group of animals that mostly lay eggs and have scaly skin

spring (SPRING) a place where fresh water bubbles up out of the ground

tropics (TRAH-piks) a warm, sunny region around the middle of the earth

FIND OUT MORE

BOOKS

Marsh, Laura. *National Geographic Kids: Sea Turtles*. Washington, DC: National Geographic, 2011.

Rhodes, Mary Jo, with David Hall. *Sea Turtles*. Danbury, CT: Children's Press, 2006.

WEB SITES

National Aquarium—Spring Cleaning: It Even Happens in the Ocean!
www.aqua.org/blog/2014/may/spring-cleaning-it-even-happens-in
-the-ocean

PBS Kids—DragonflyTV: Sea Turtles by Devin and Zach
http://pbskids.org/dragonflytv/show/seaturtles.html

Waikiki Aquarium: Yellow Tang
www.waikikiaquarium.org/experience/animal-guide/fishes
/surgeonfishes/yellow-tang

INDEX

ABOUT THE AUTHOR

Kevin Cunningham has written more than 60 books. He lives near Chicago.